ANIMALS GETTING HIGH

Adult coloring book

Illustrations by Aeric McBride

ANIMALS GETTING HIGH

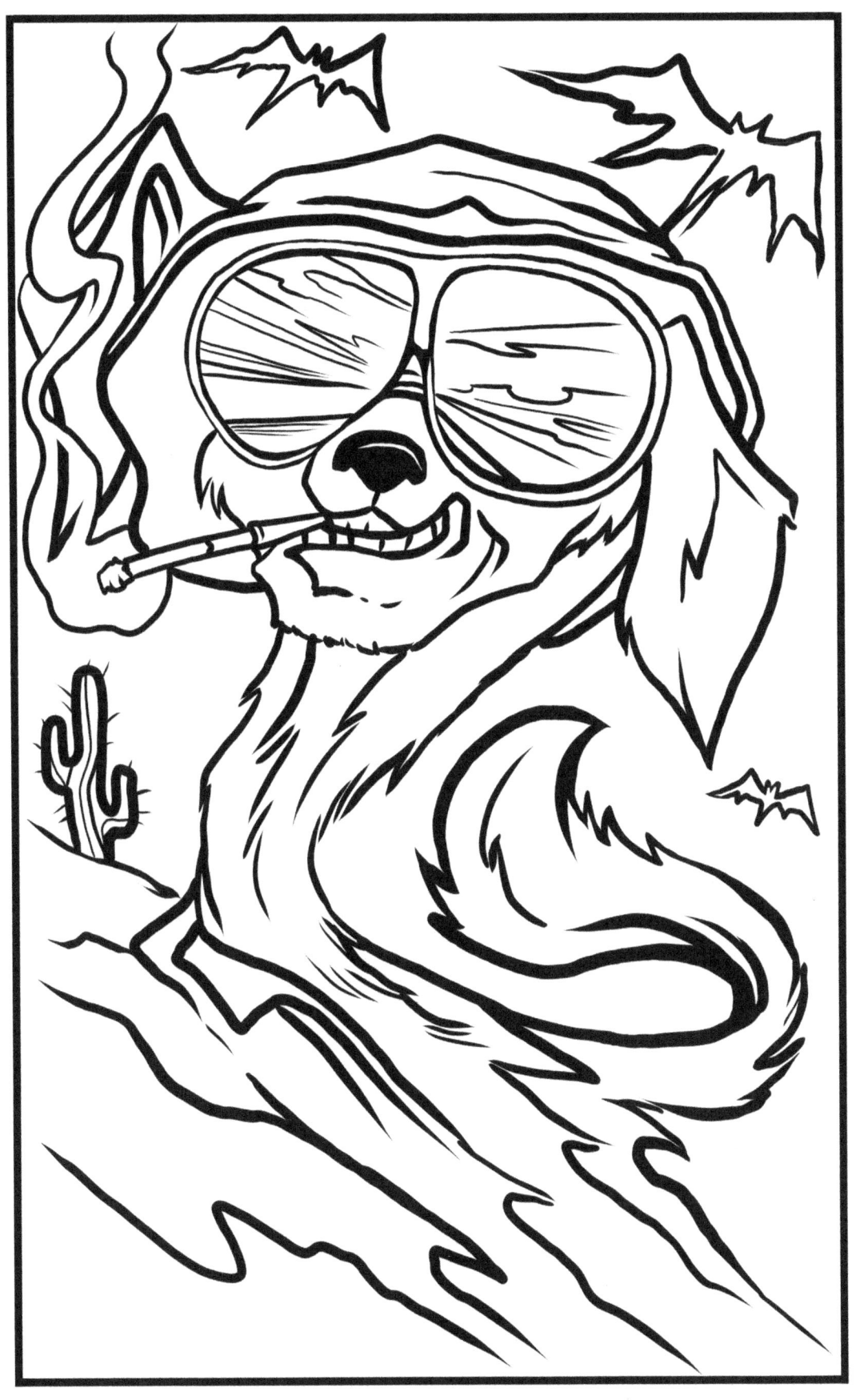

ANIMALS GETTING HIGH

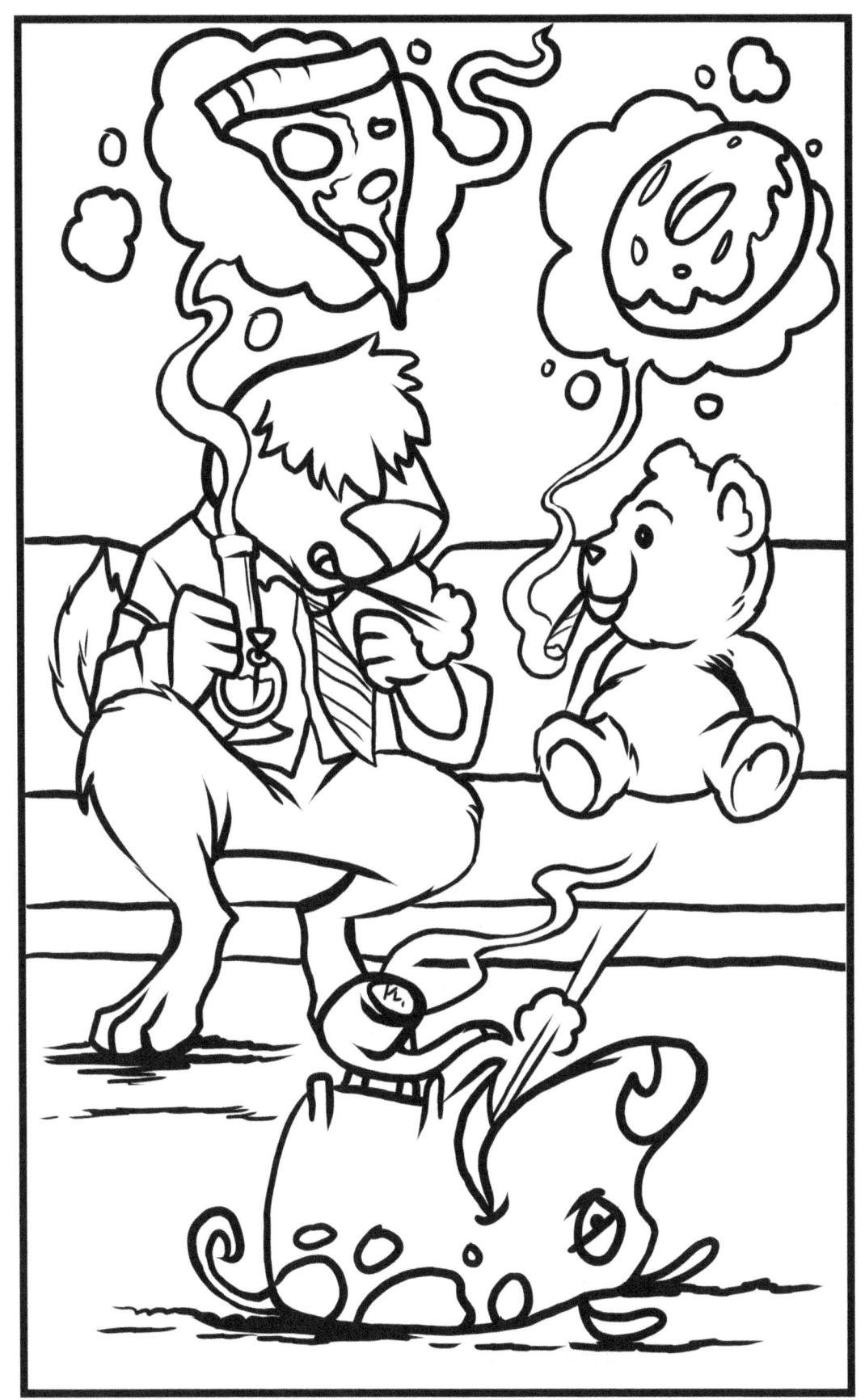

ANIMALS GETTING HIGH

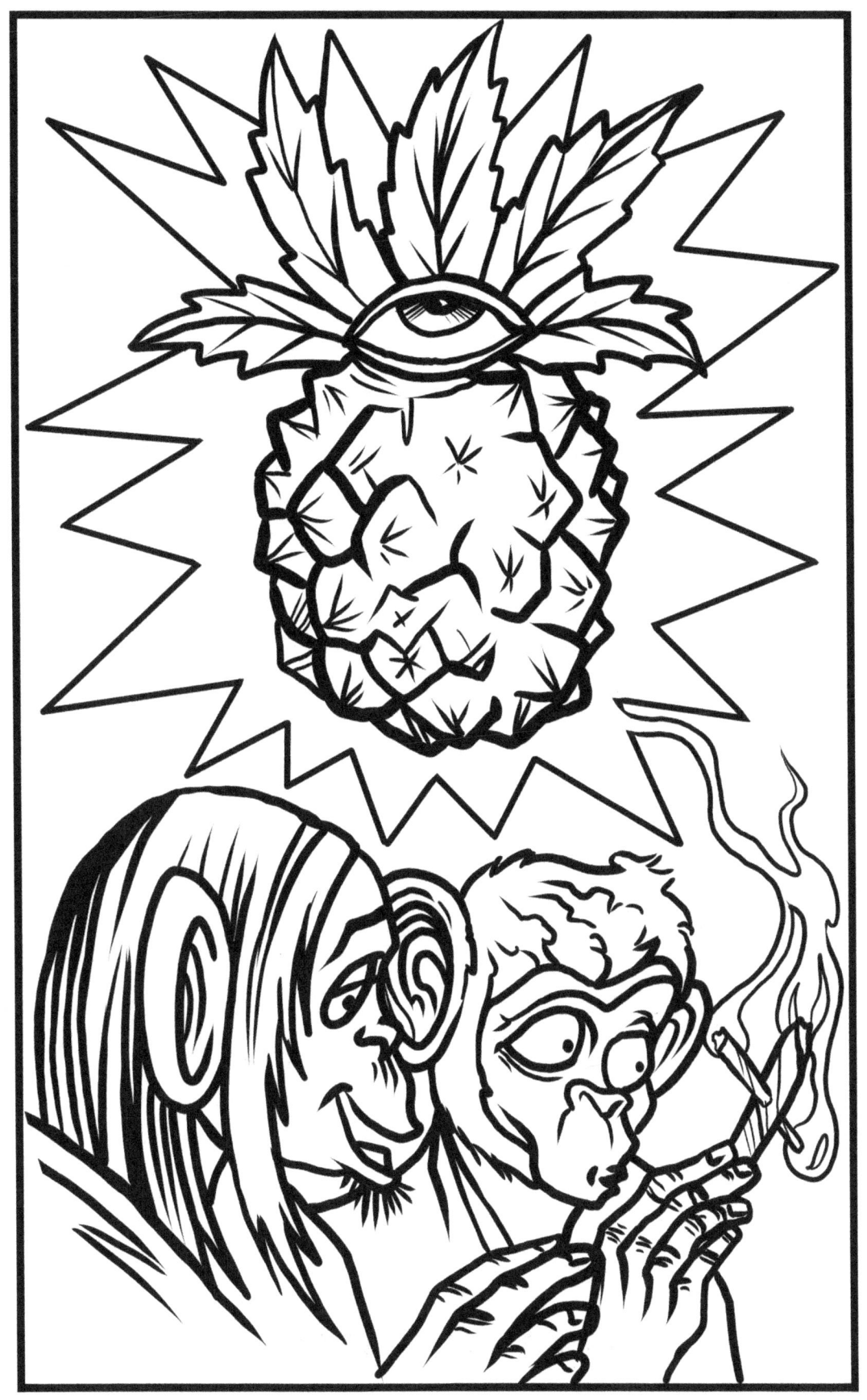

ANIMALS GETTING HIGH

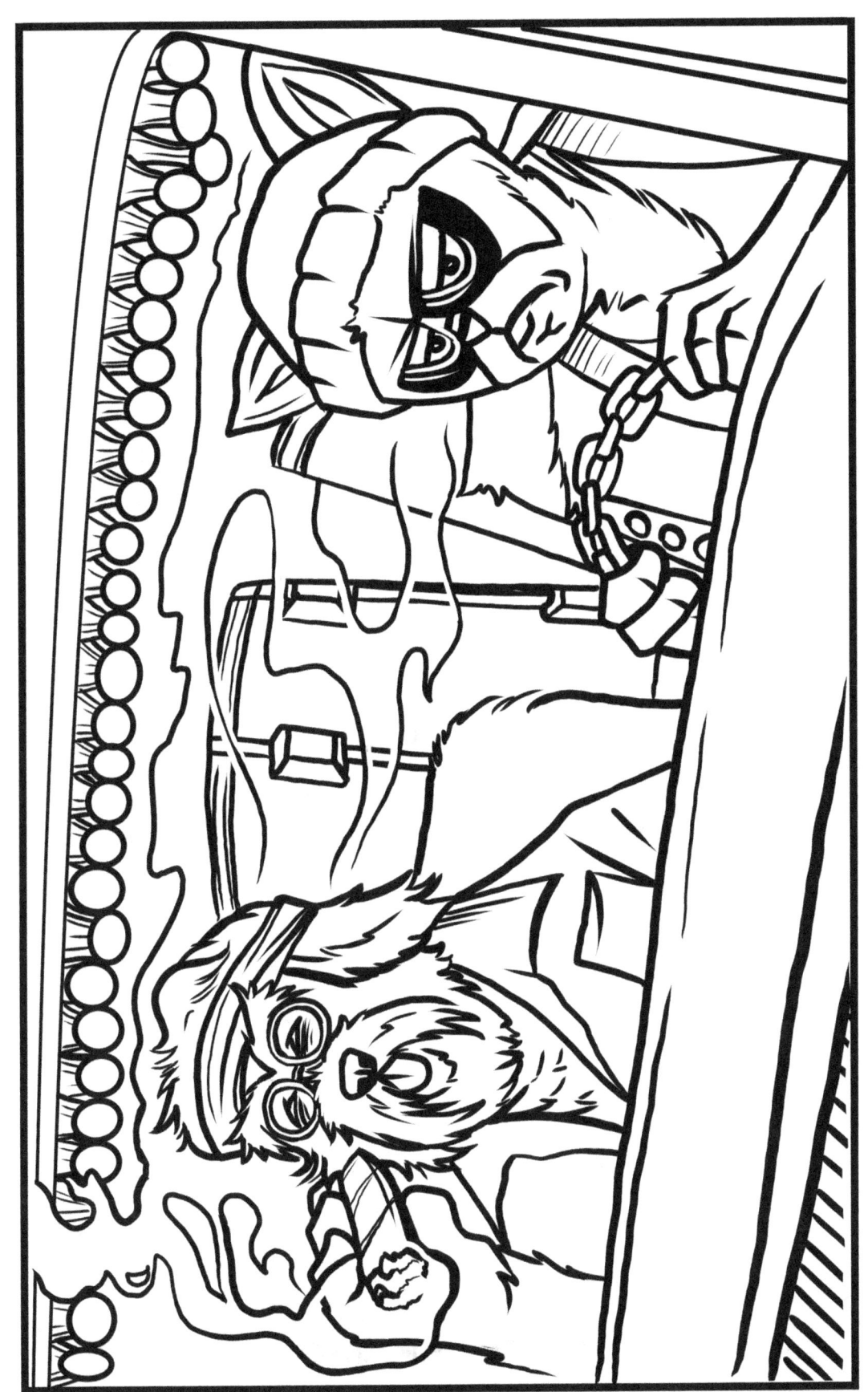

ANIMALS GETTING HIGH

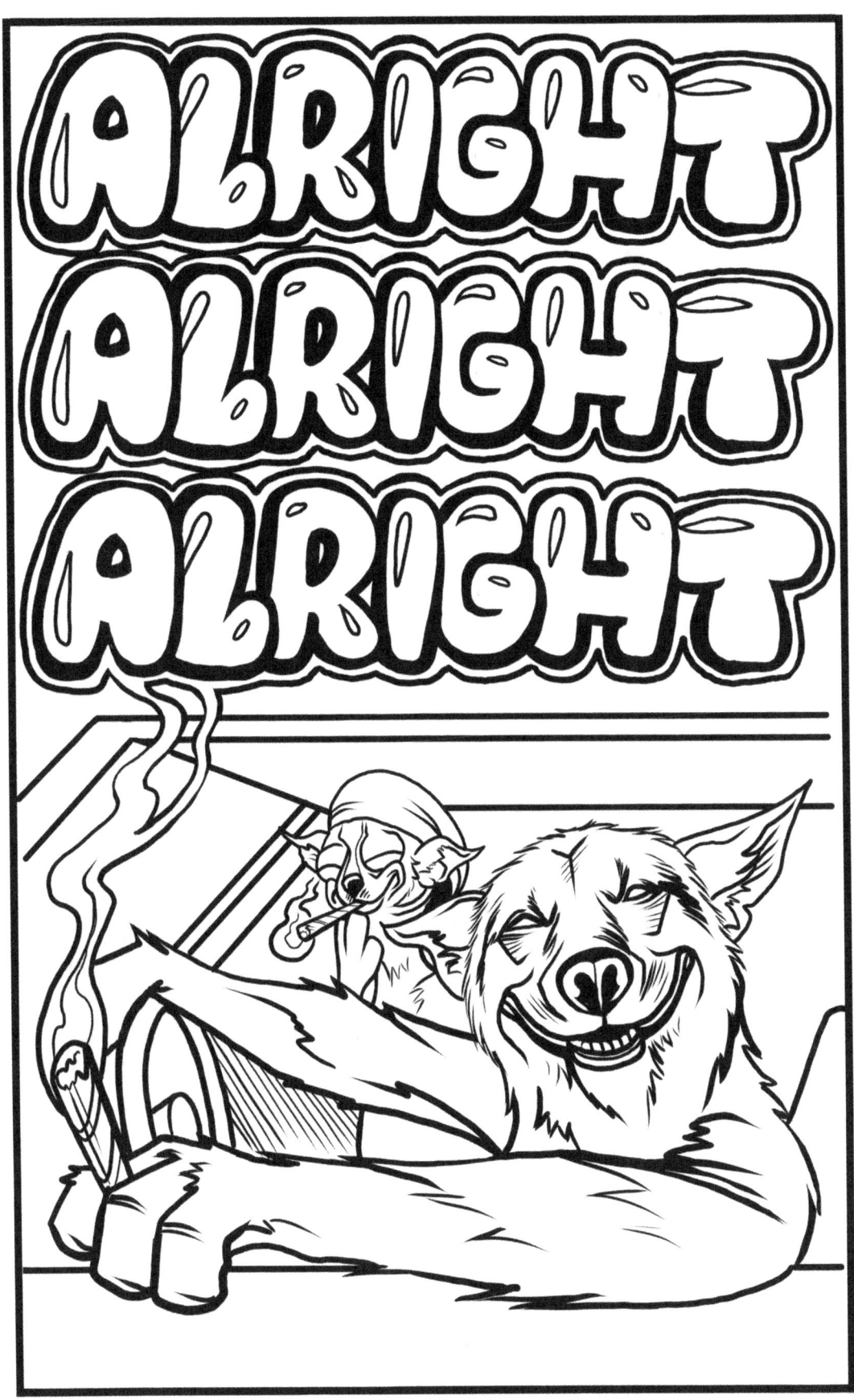

ANIMALS GETTING HIGH

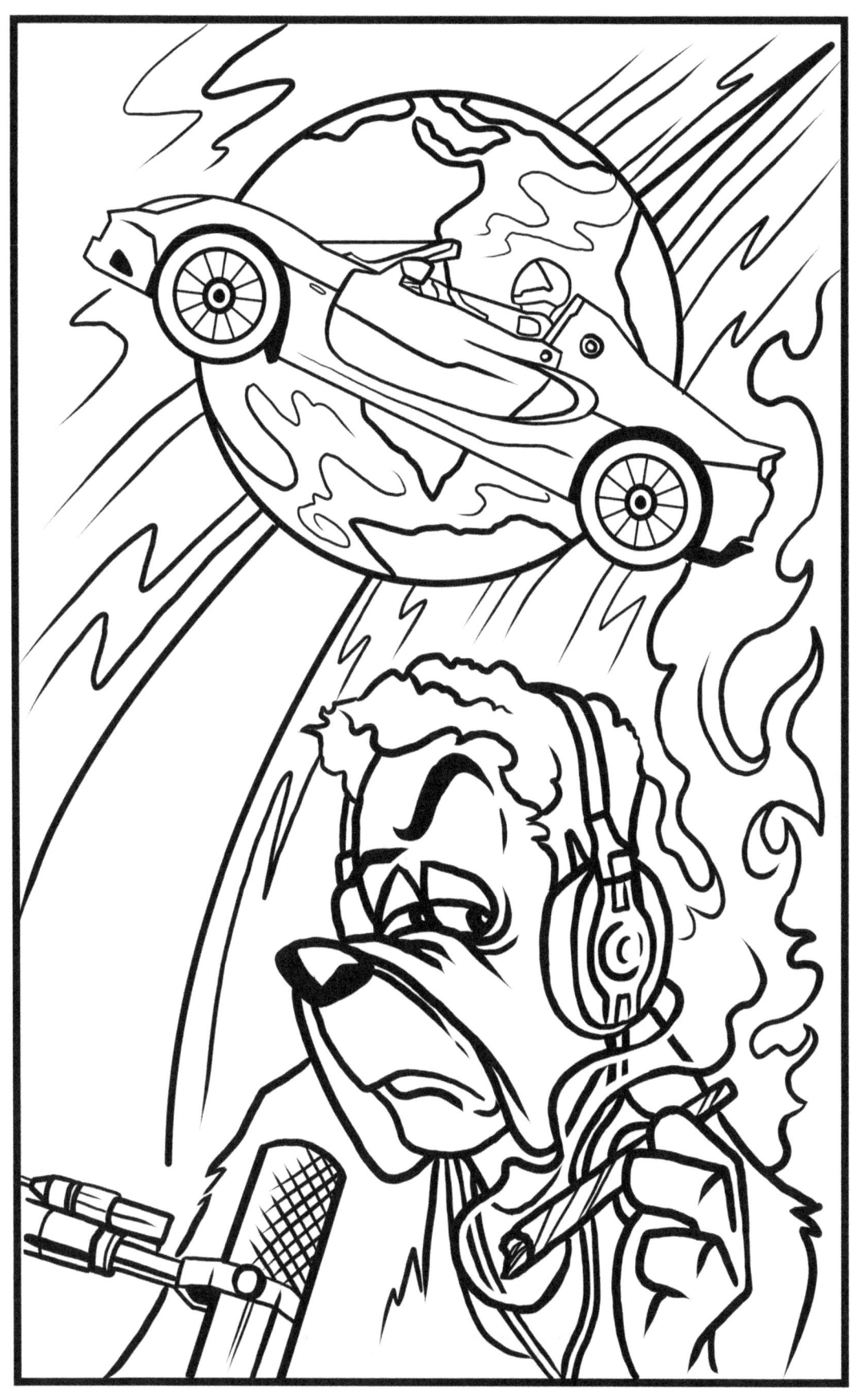

ANIMALS GETTING HIGH

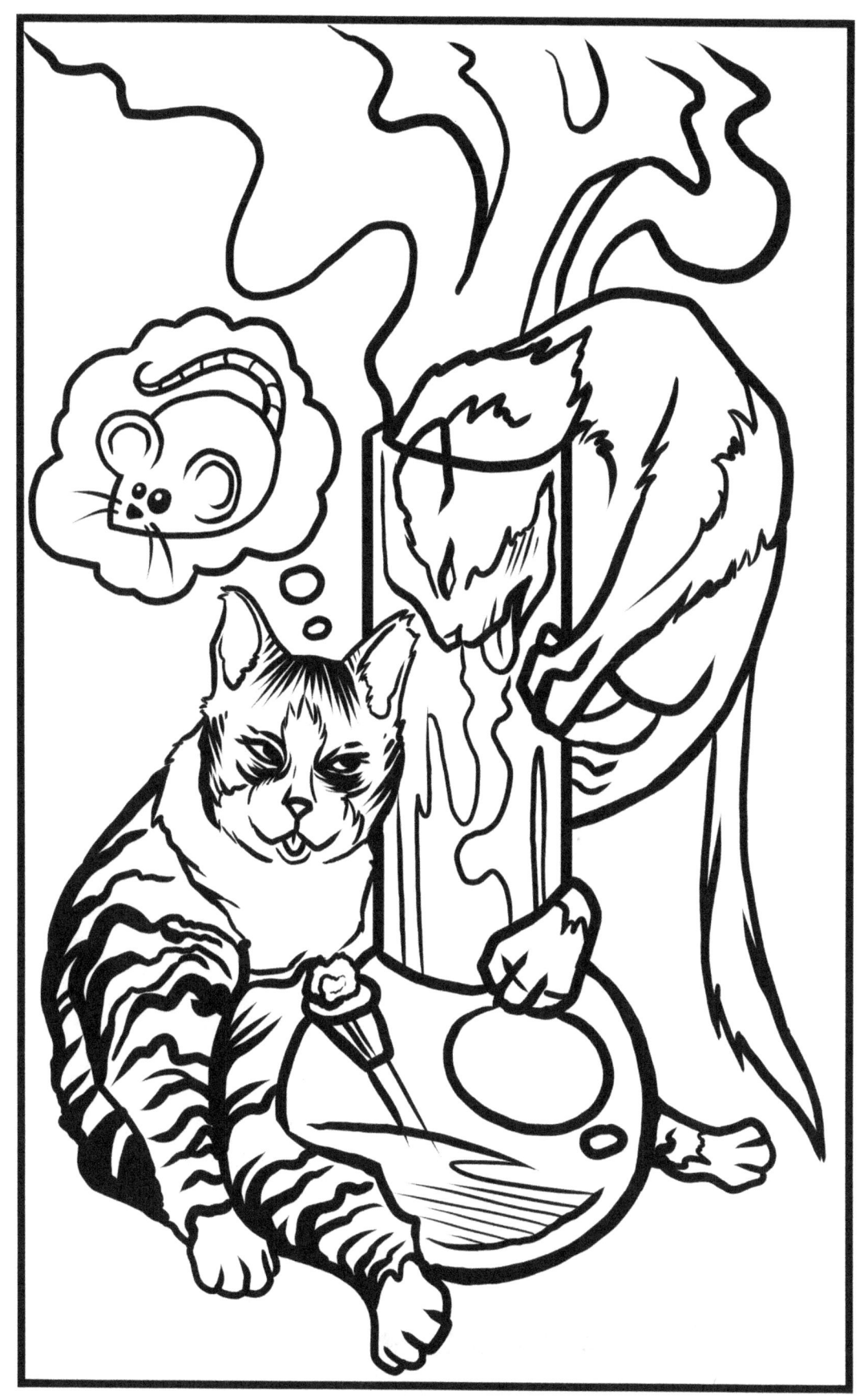

ANIMALS GETTING HIGH

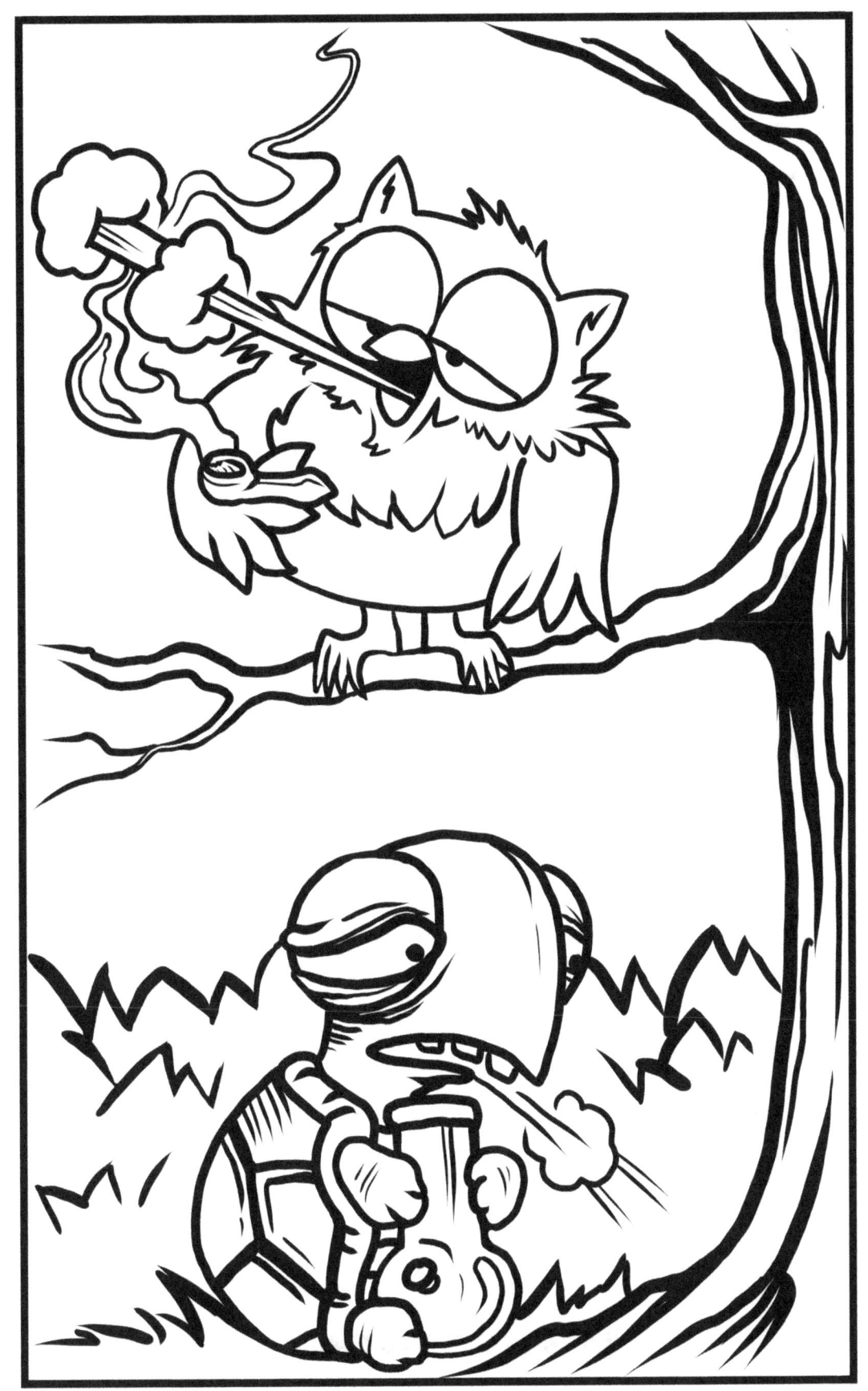

ANIMALS GETTING HIGH

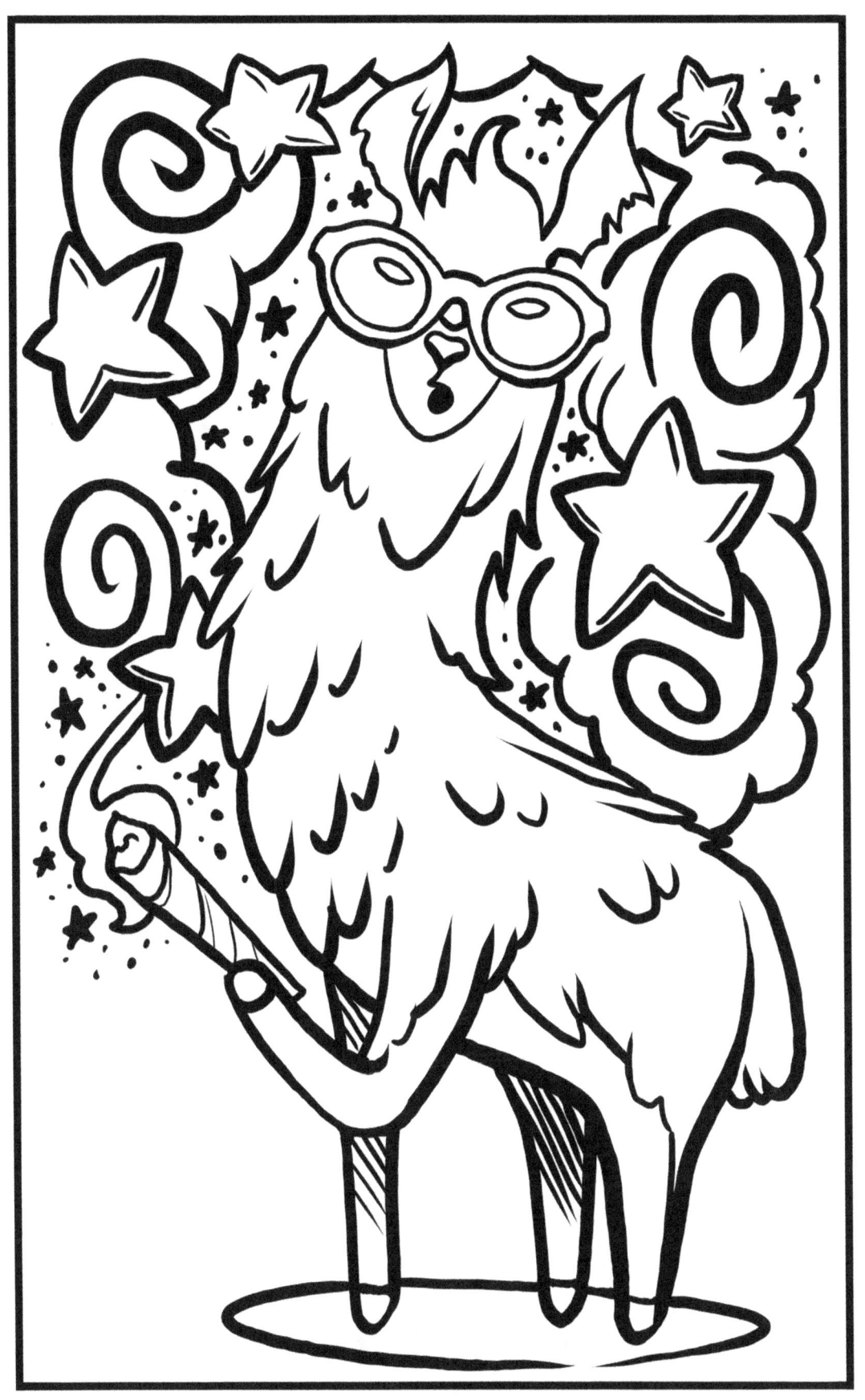

ANIMALS GETTING HIGH

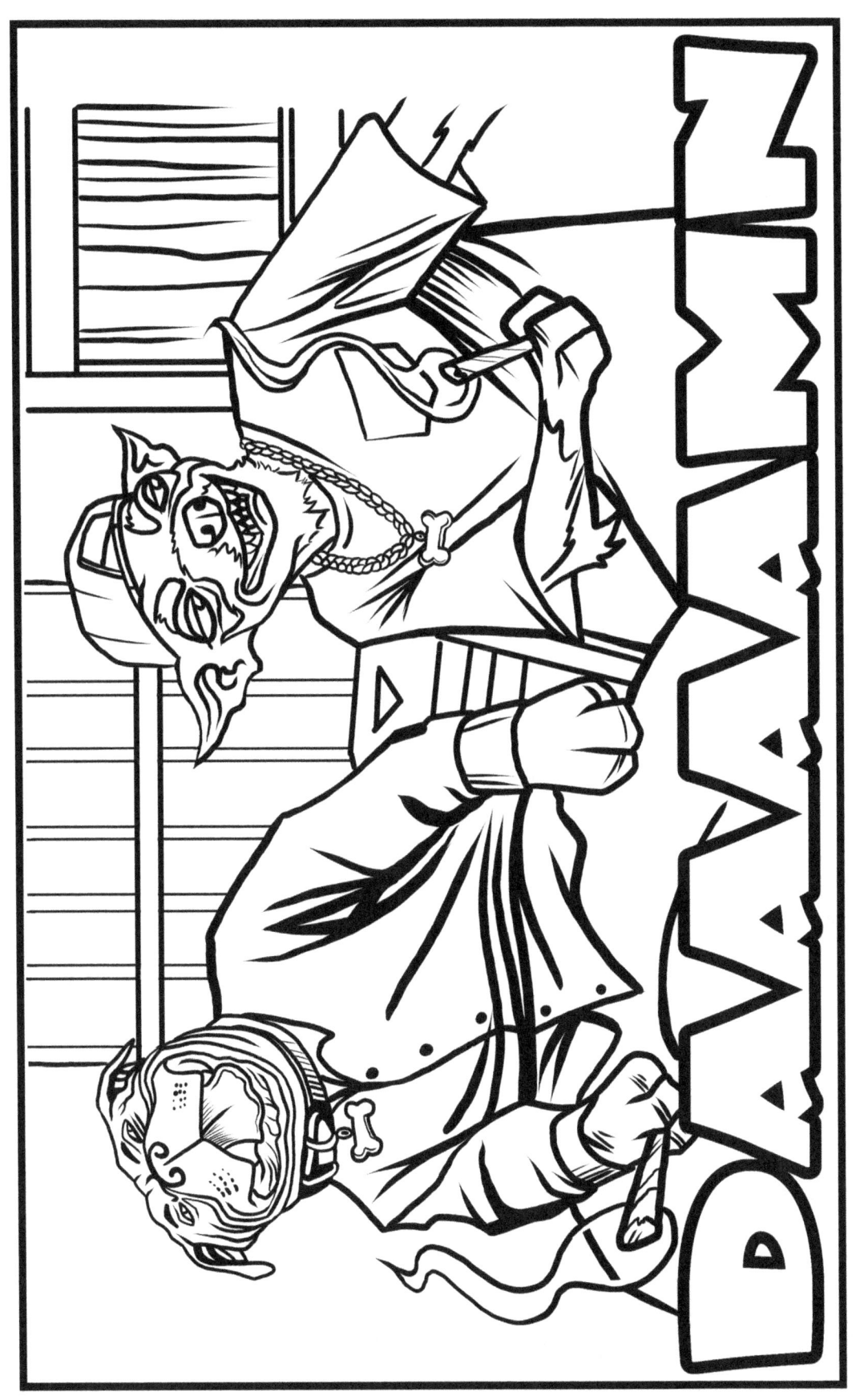

ANIMALS GETTING HIGH

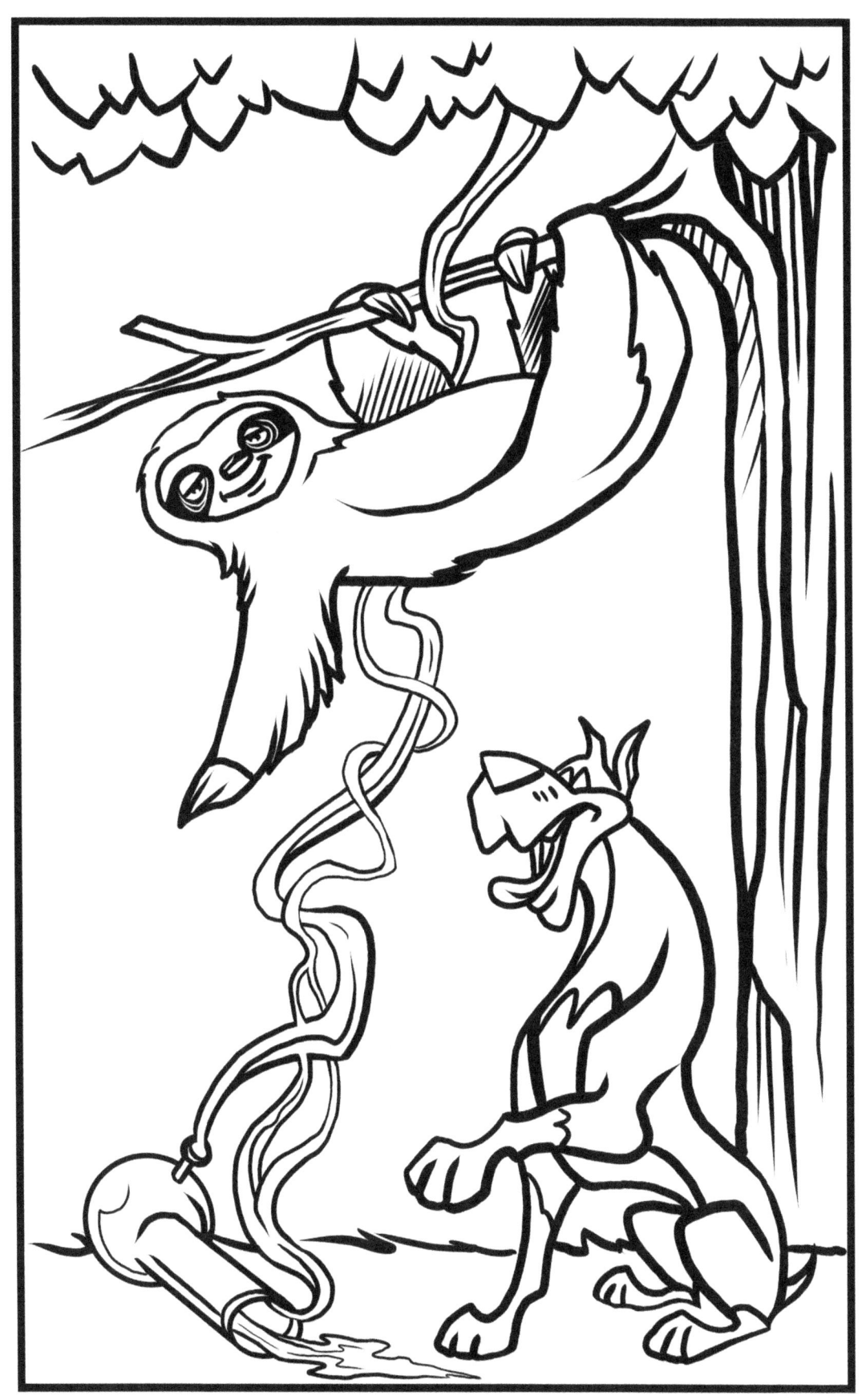

ANIMALS GETTING HIGH

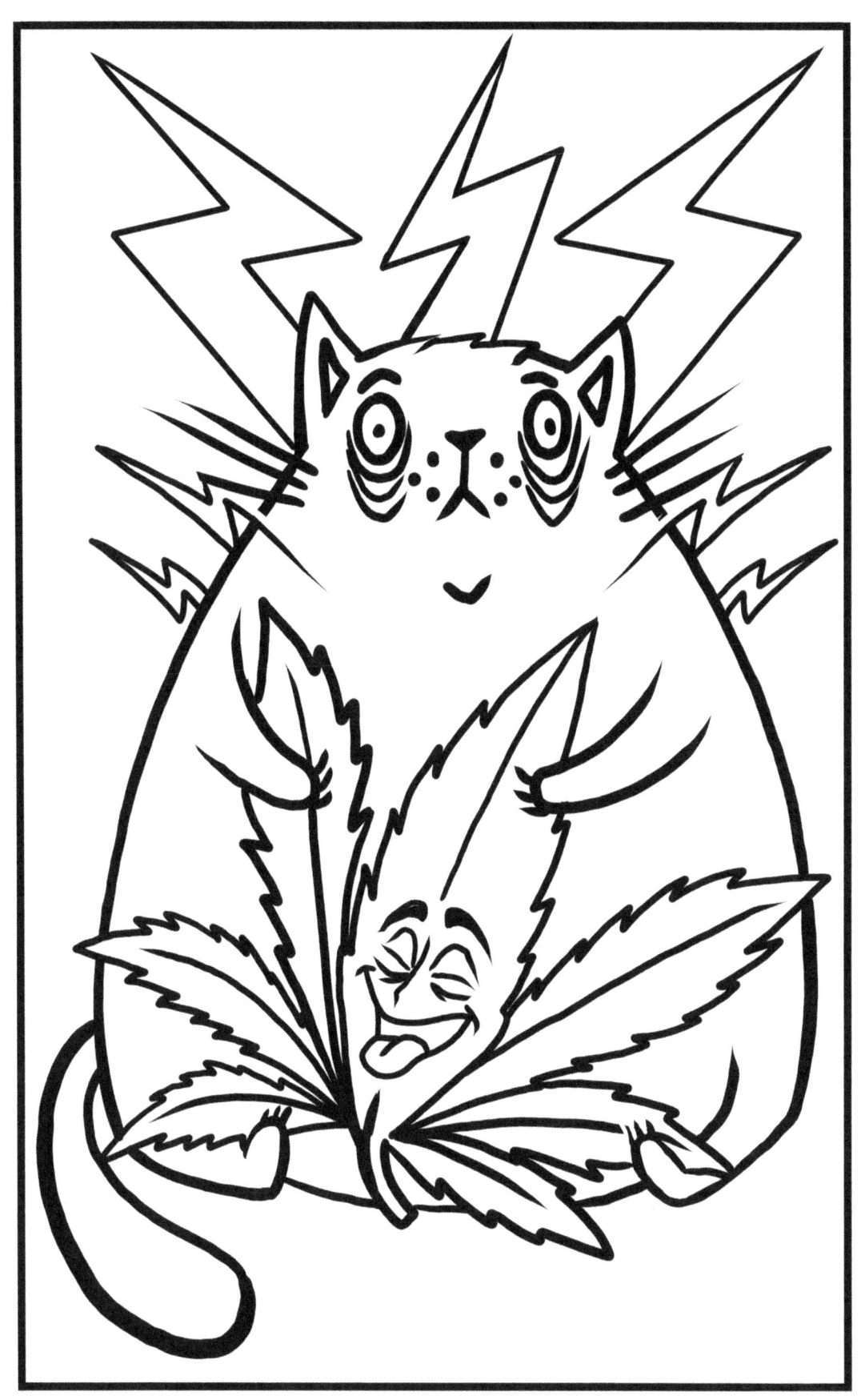

ANIMALS GETTING HIGH

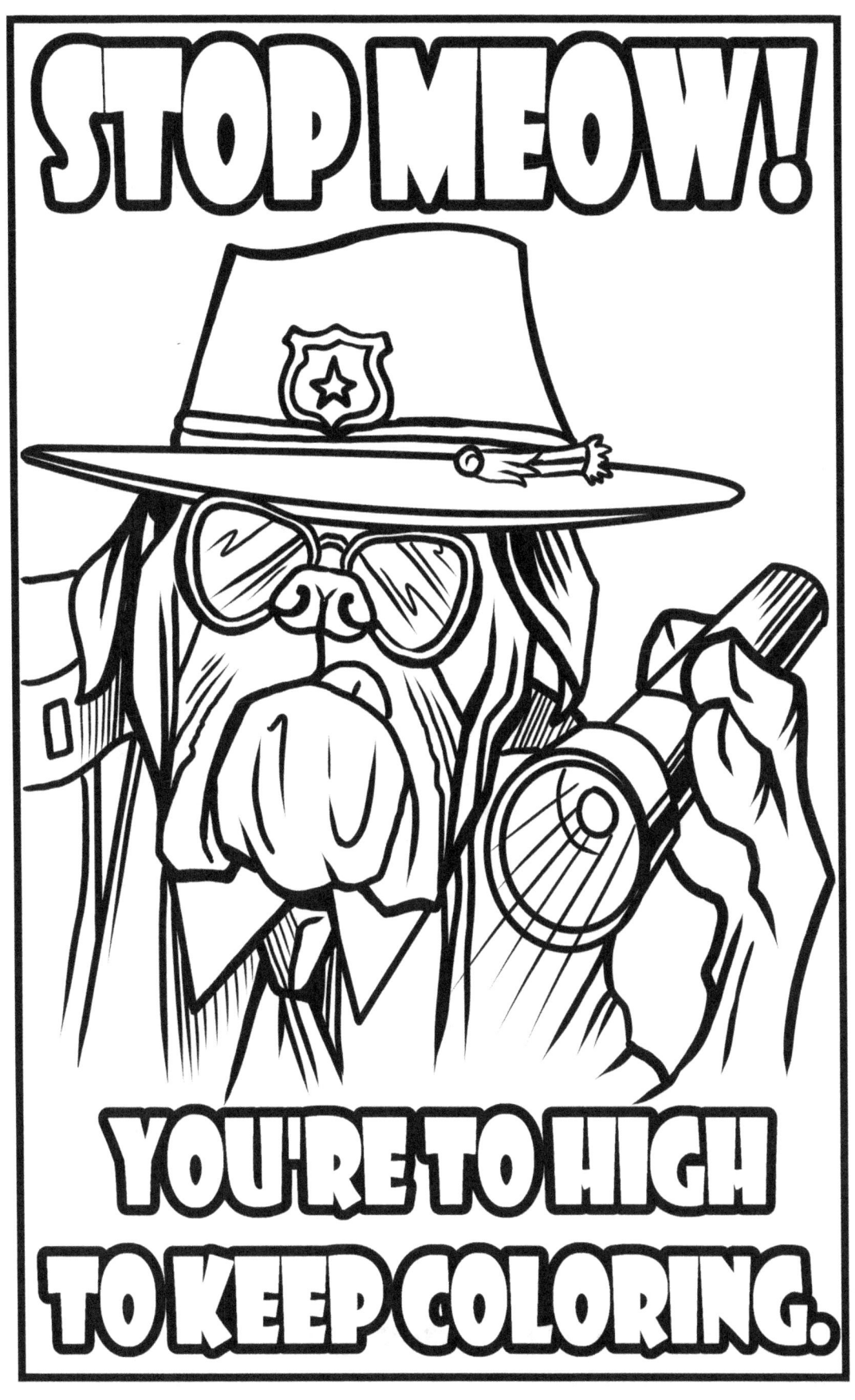

ANIMALS GETTING HIGH

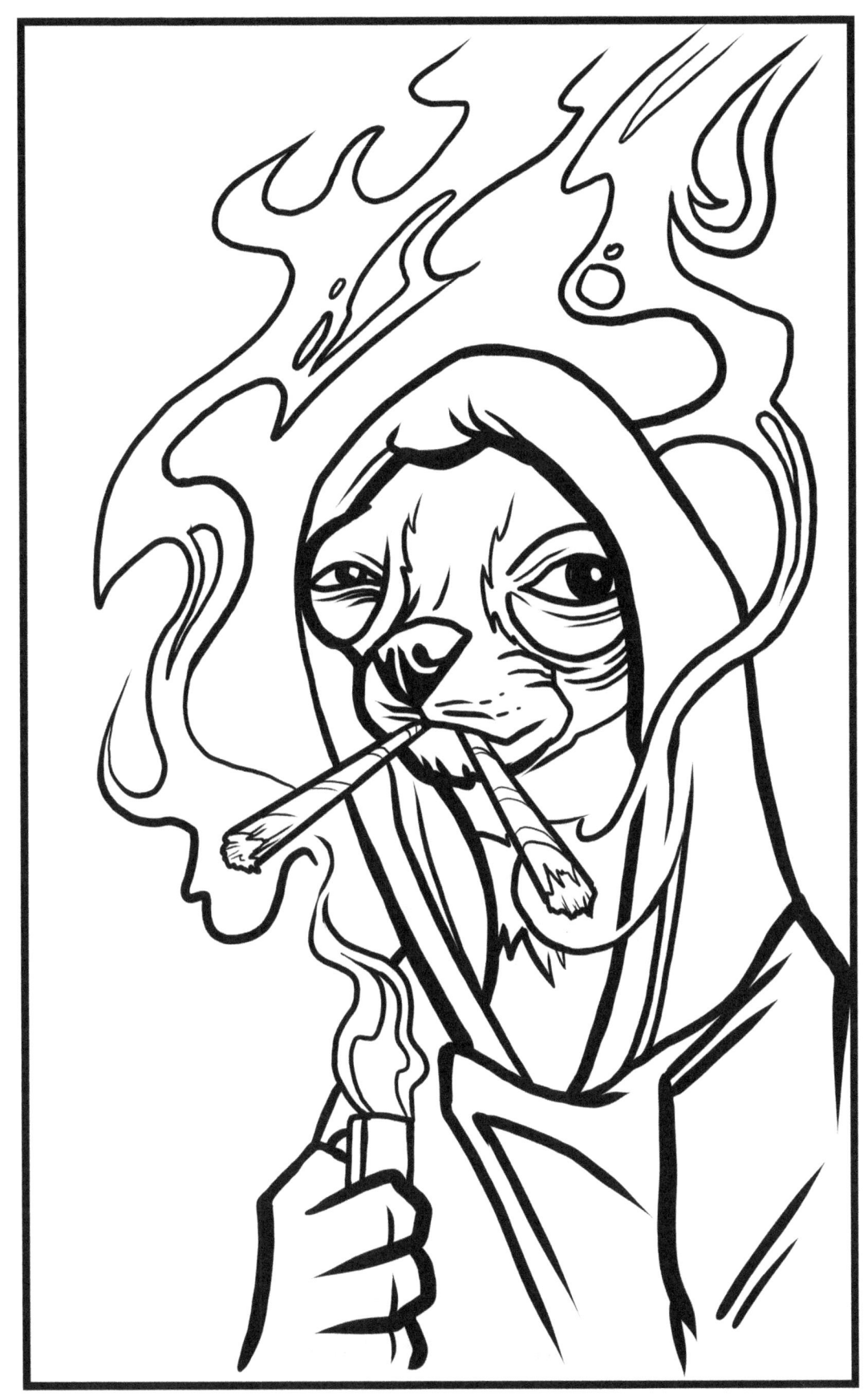

ANIMALS GETTING HIGH

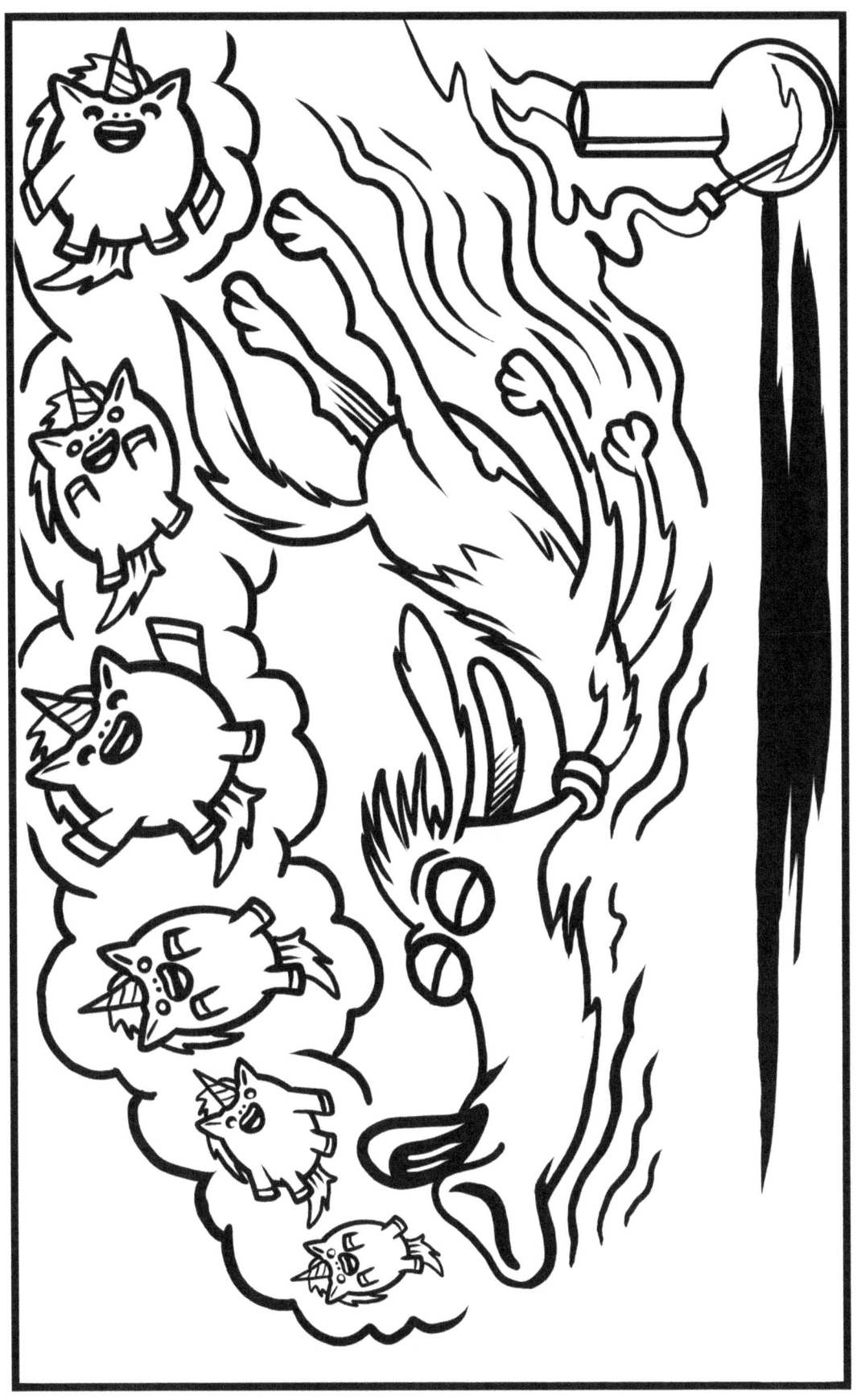

ANIMALS GETTING HIGH

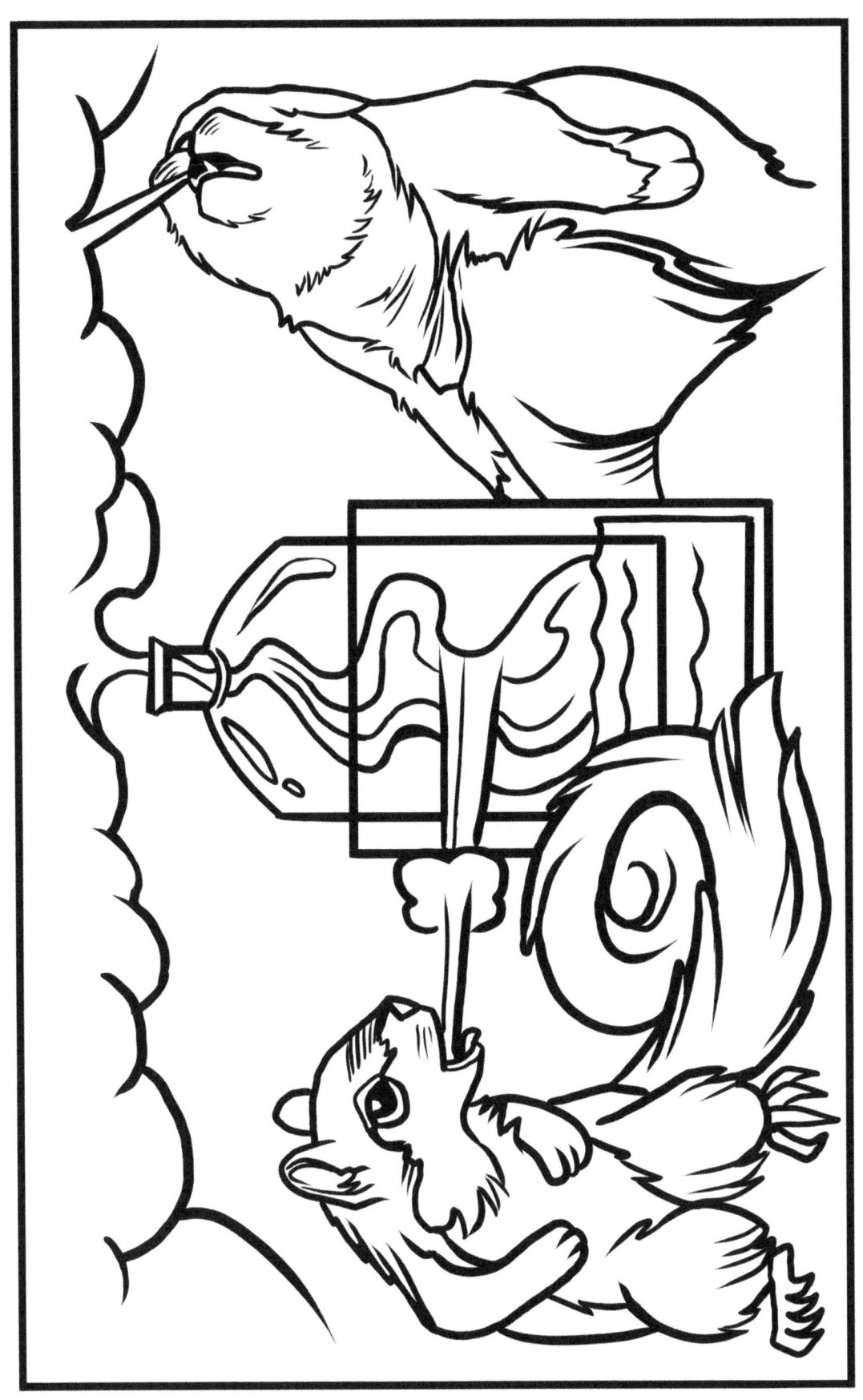

ANIMALS GETTING HIGH

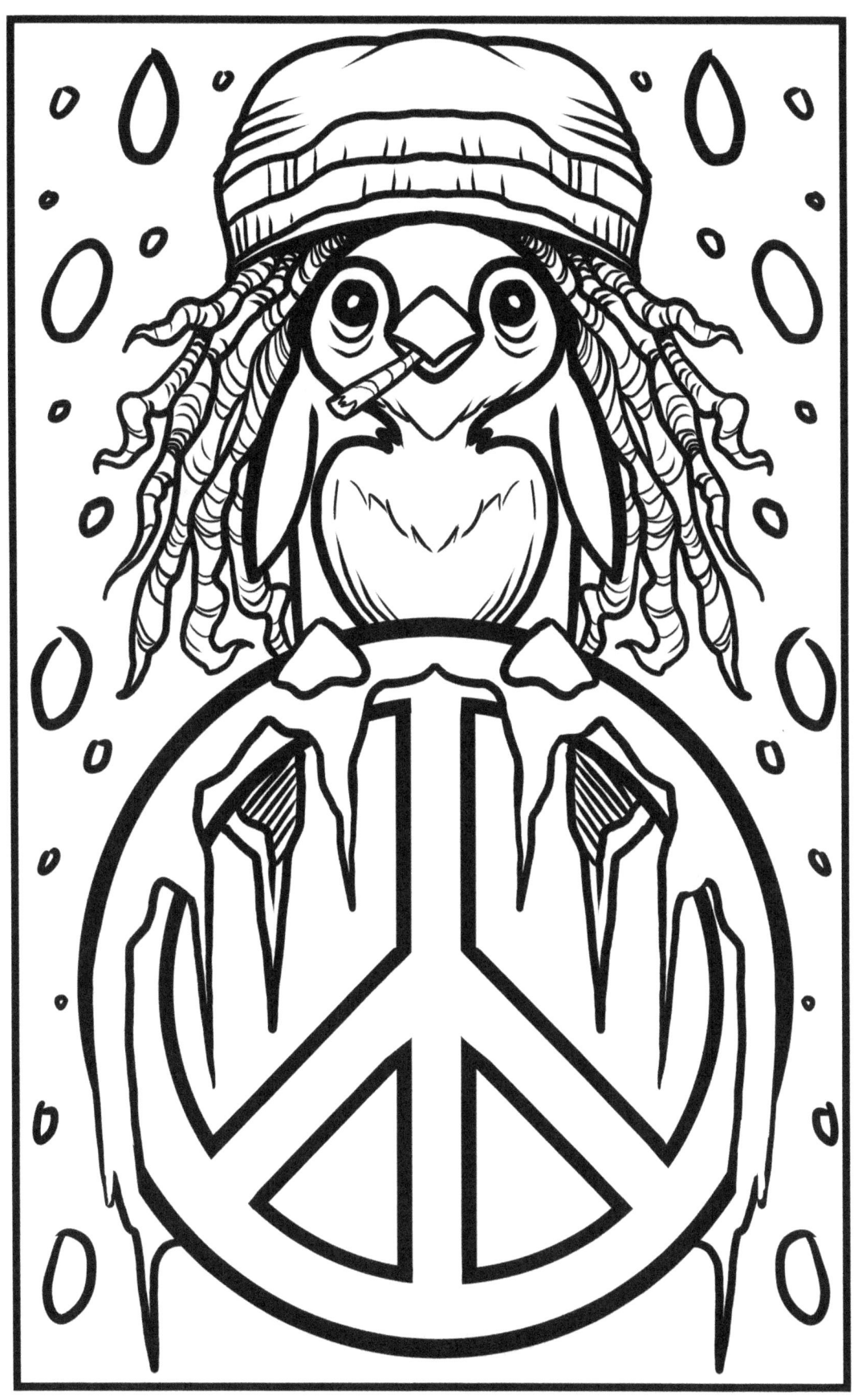

ANIMALS GETTING HIGH

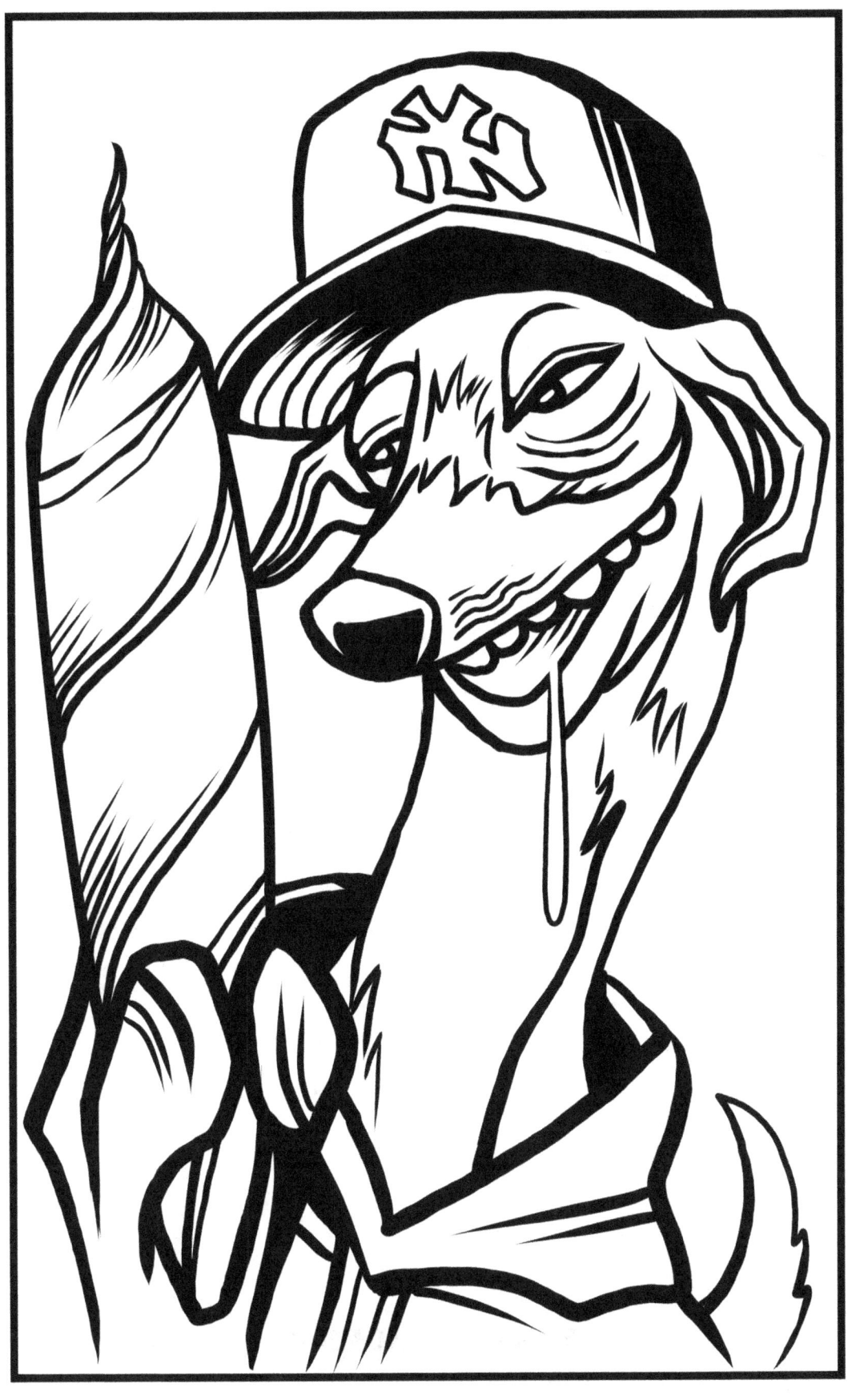

ANIMALS GETTING HIGH

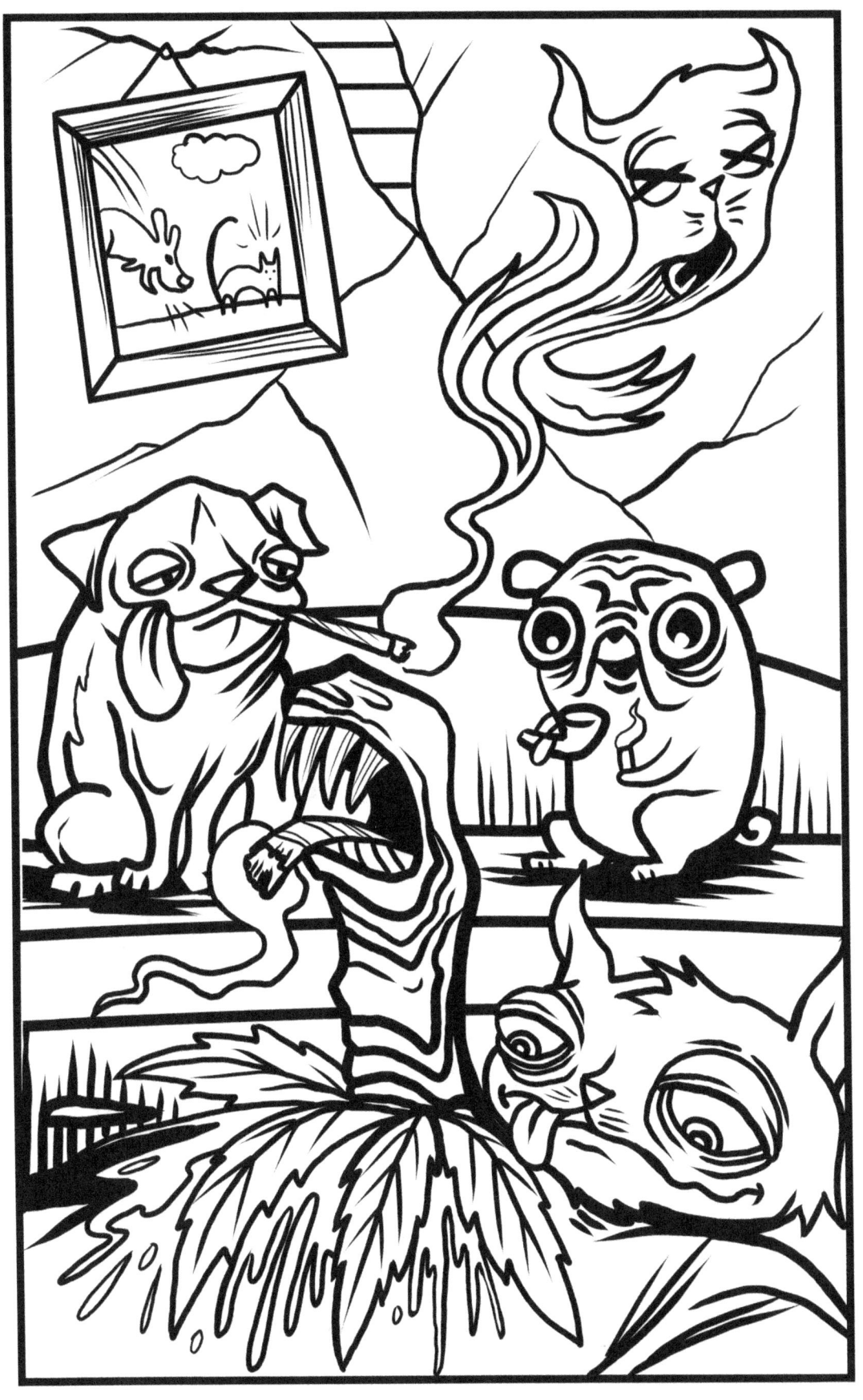

ANIMALS GETTING HIGH

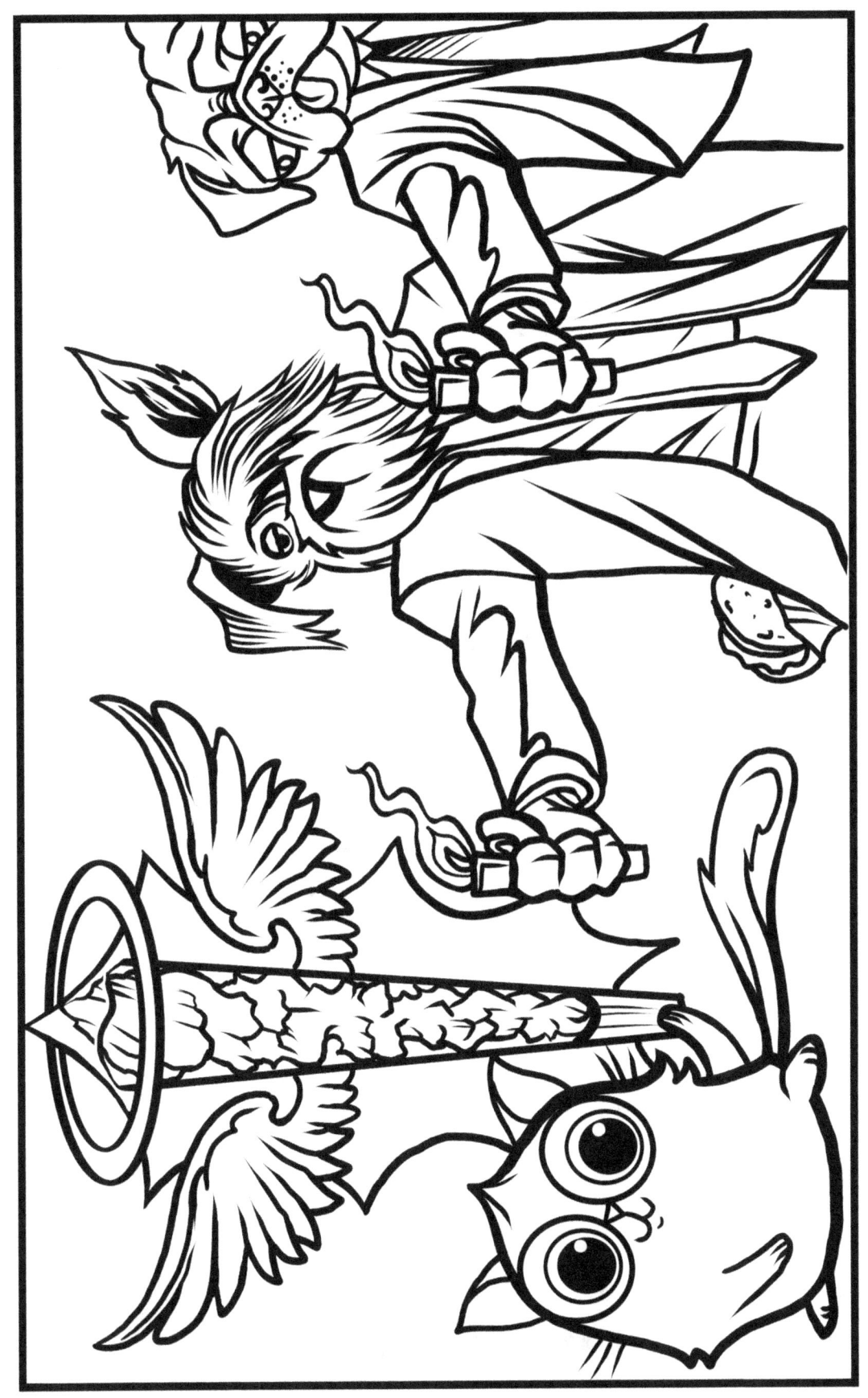

ANIMALS GETTING HIGH

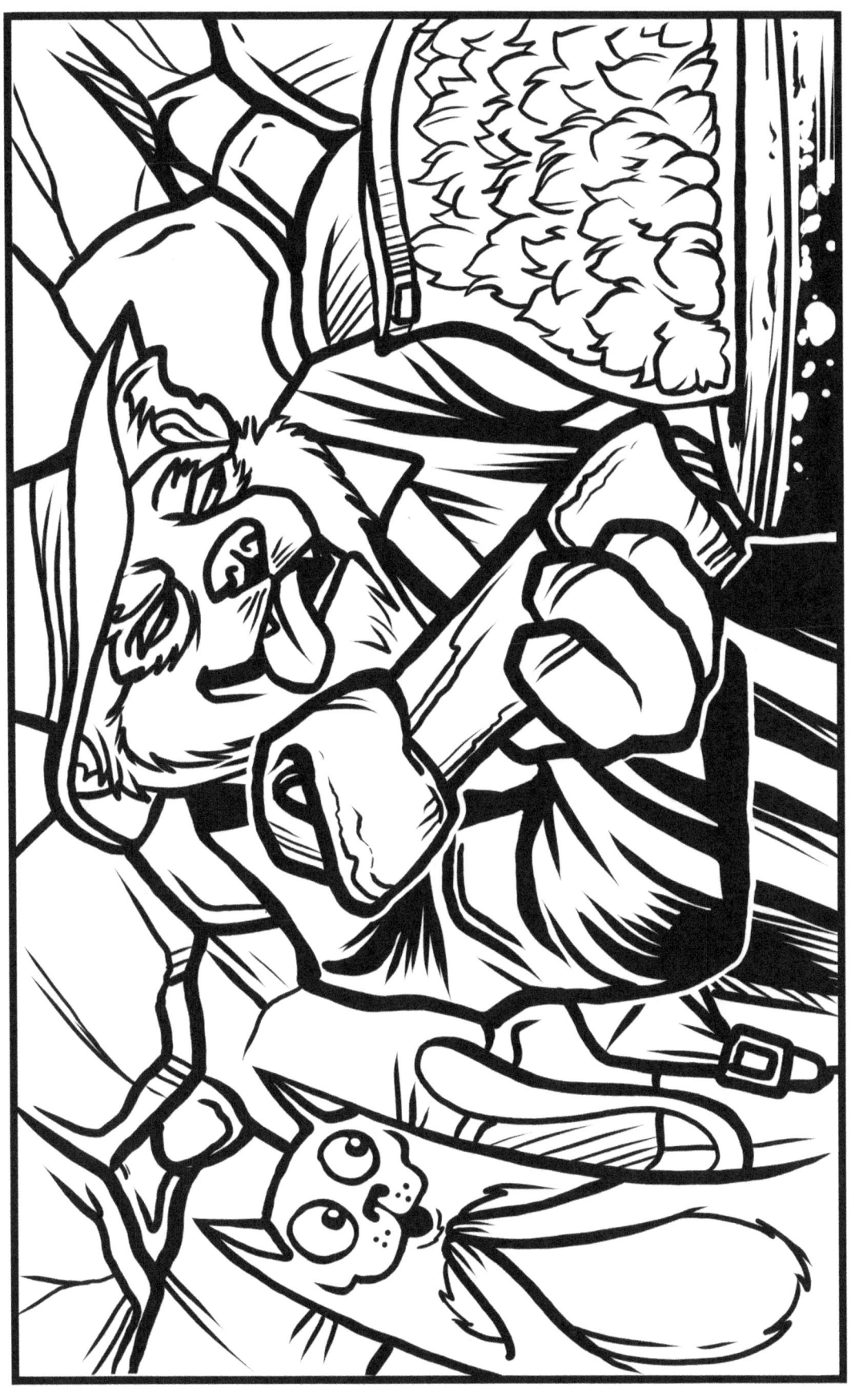

ANIMALS GETTING HIGH

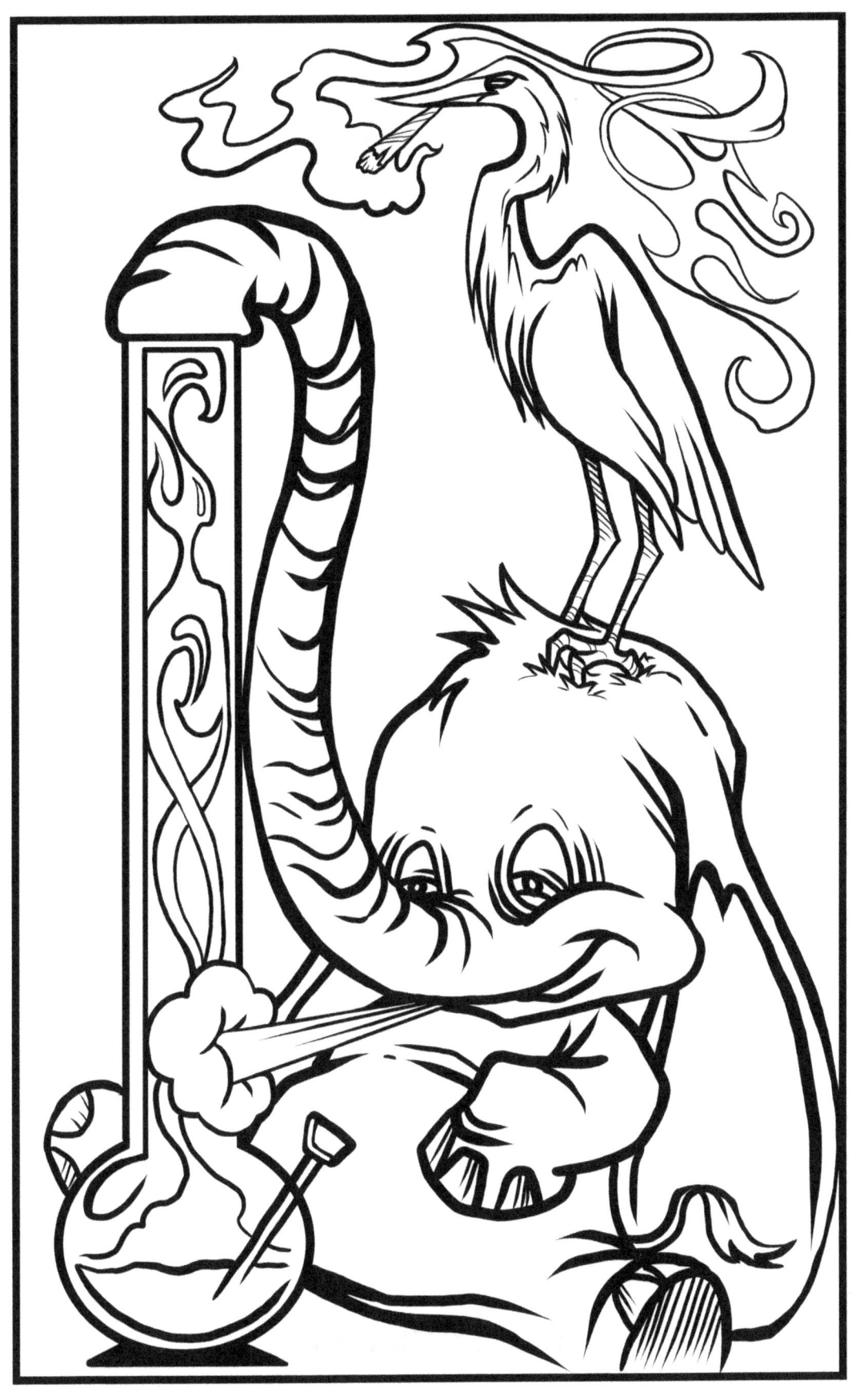

ANIMALS GETTING HIGH

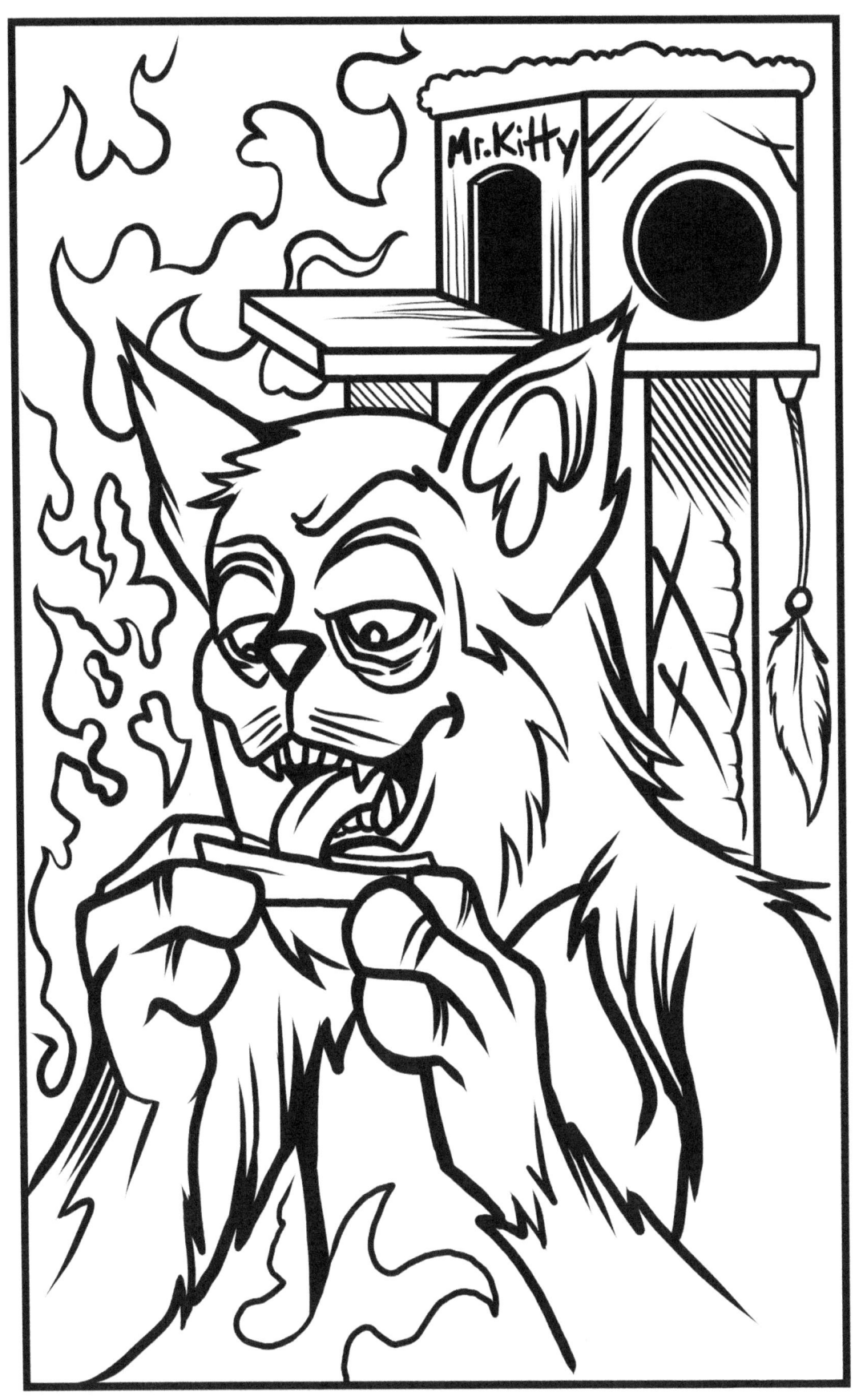

ANIMALS GETTING HIGH

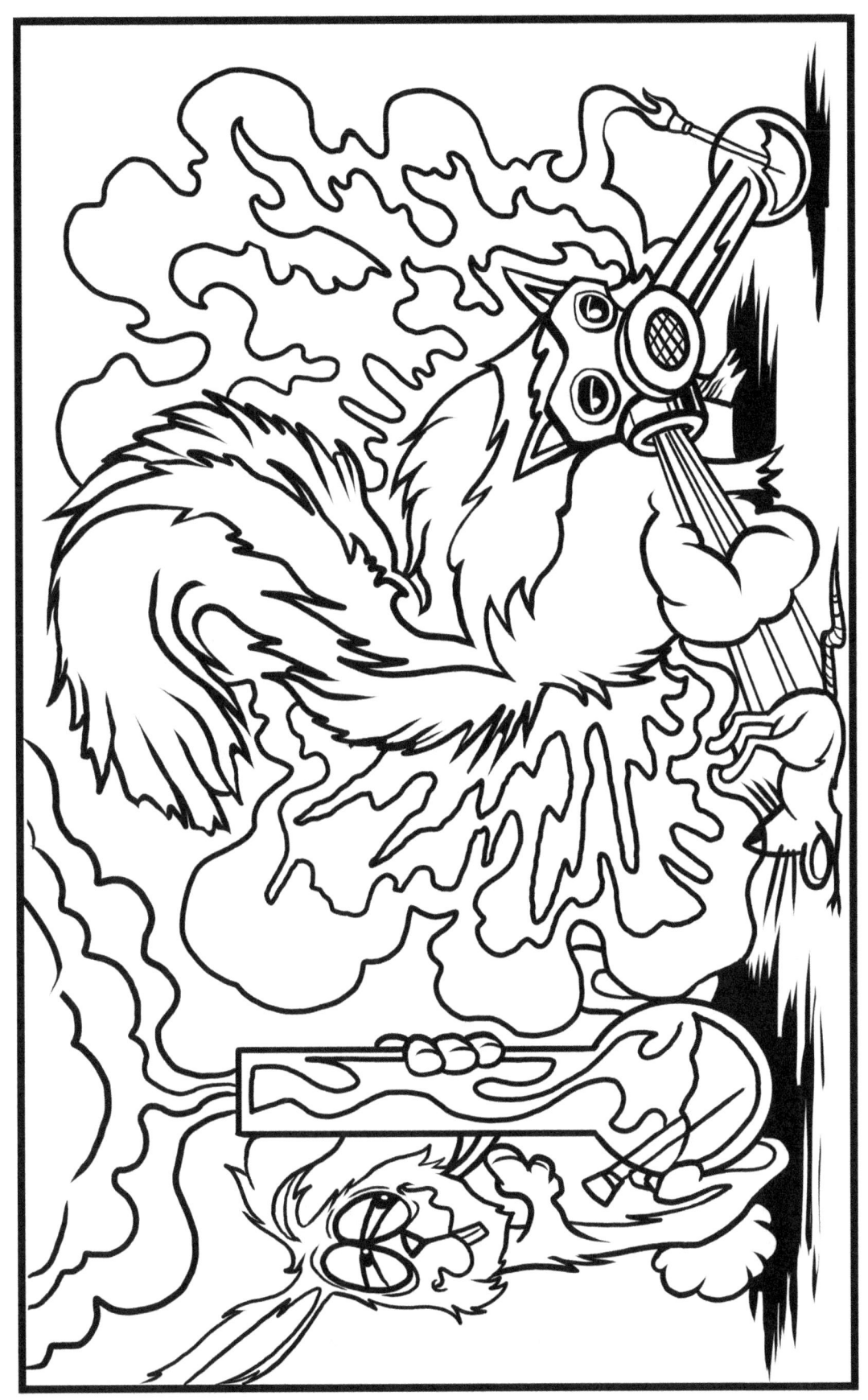

ANIMALS GETTING HIGH

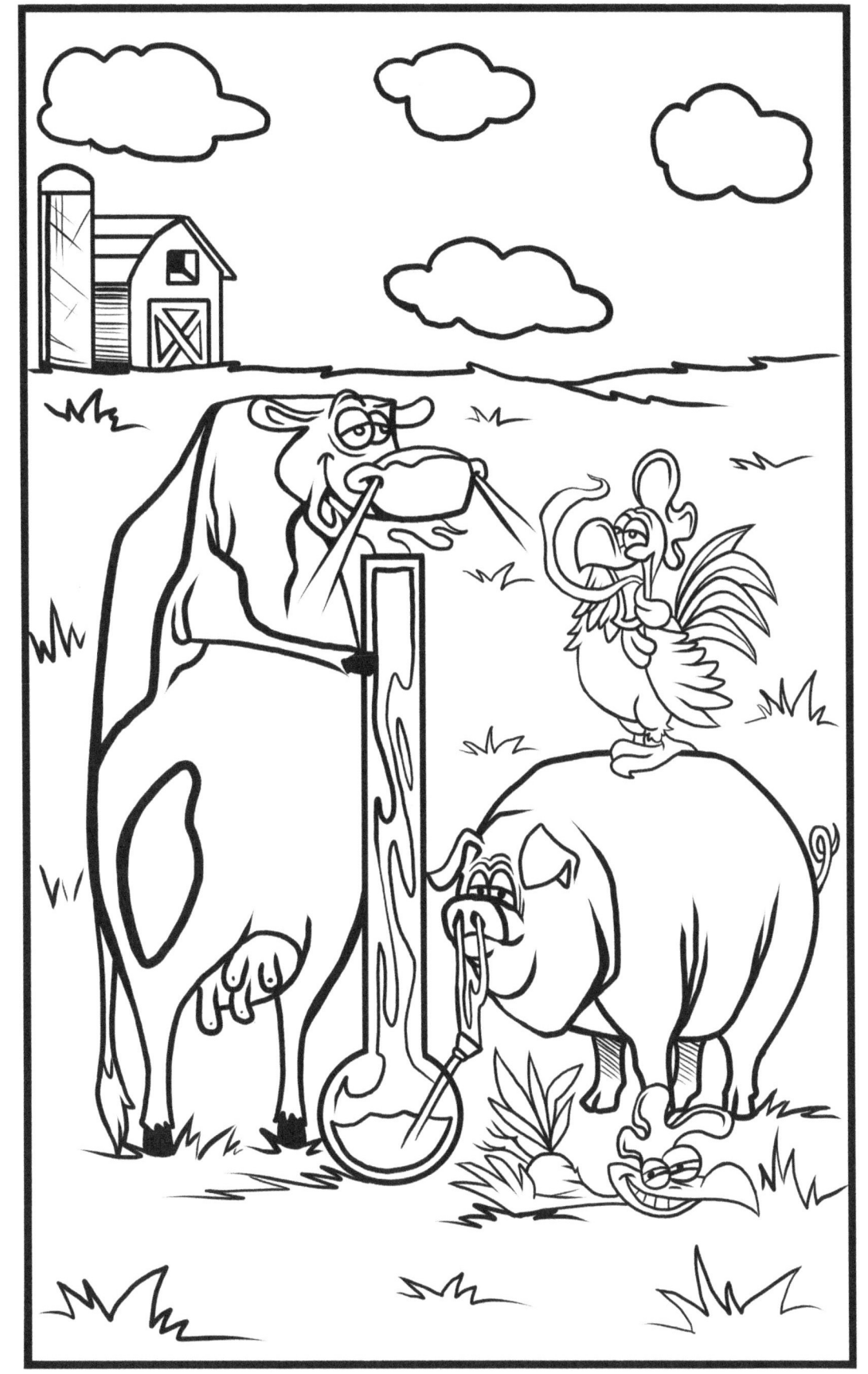

ANIMALS GETTING HIGH

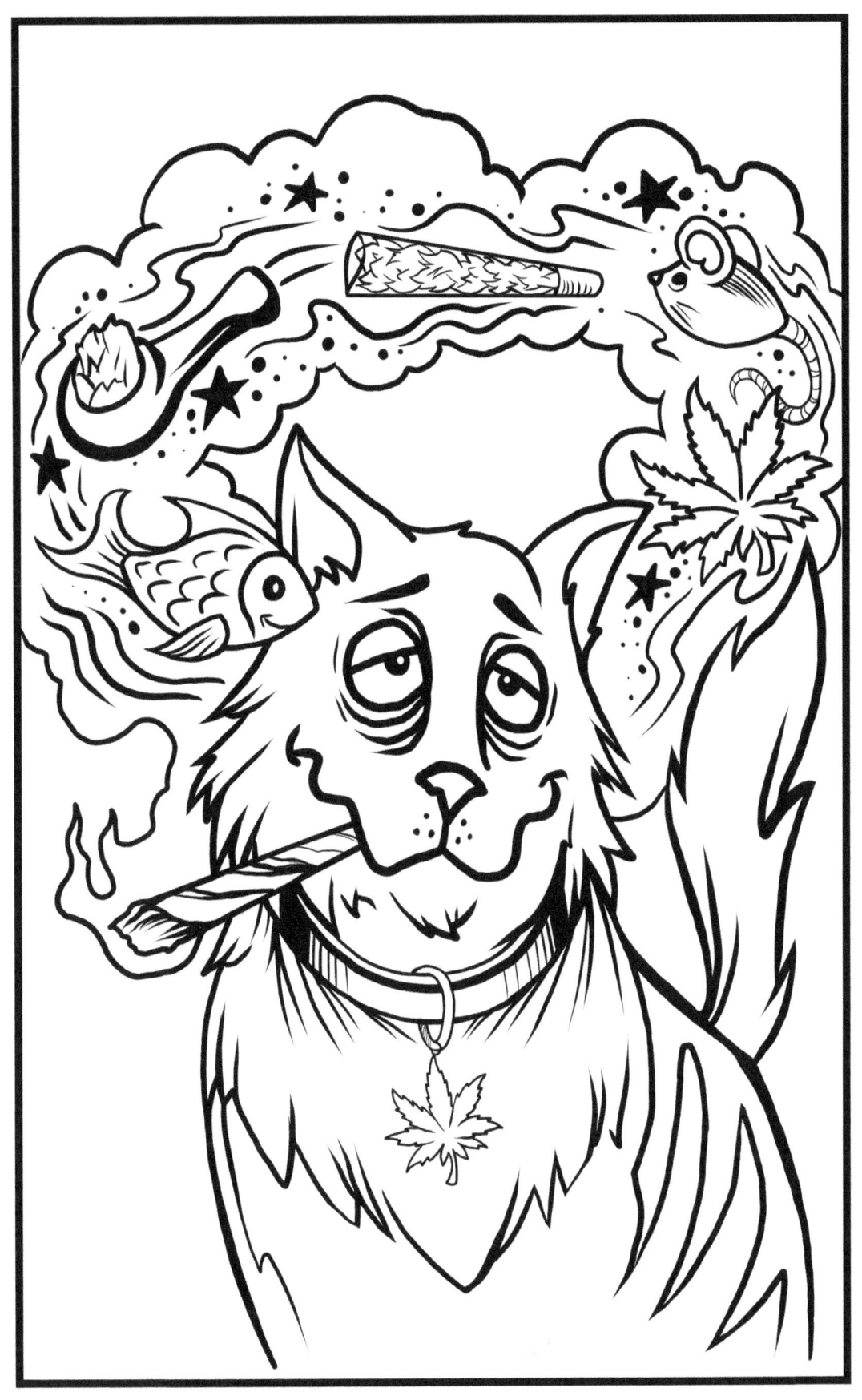

ANIMALS GETTING HIGH

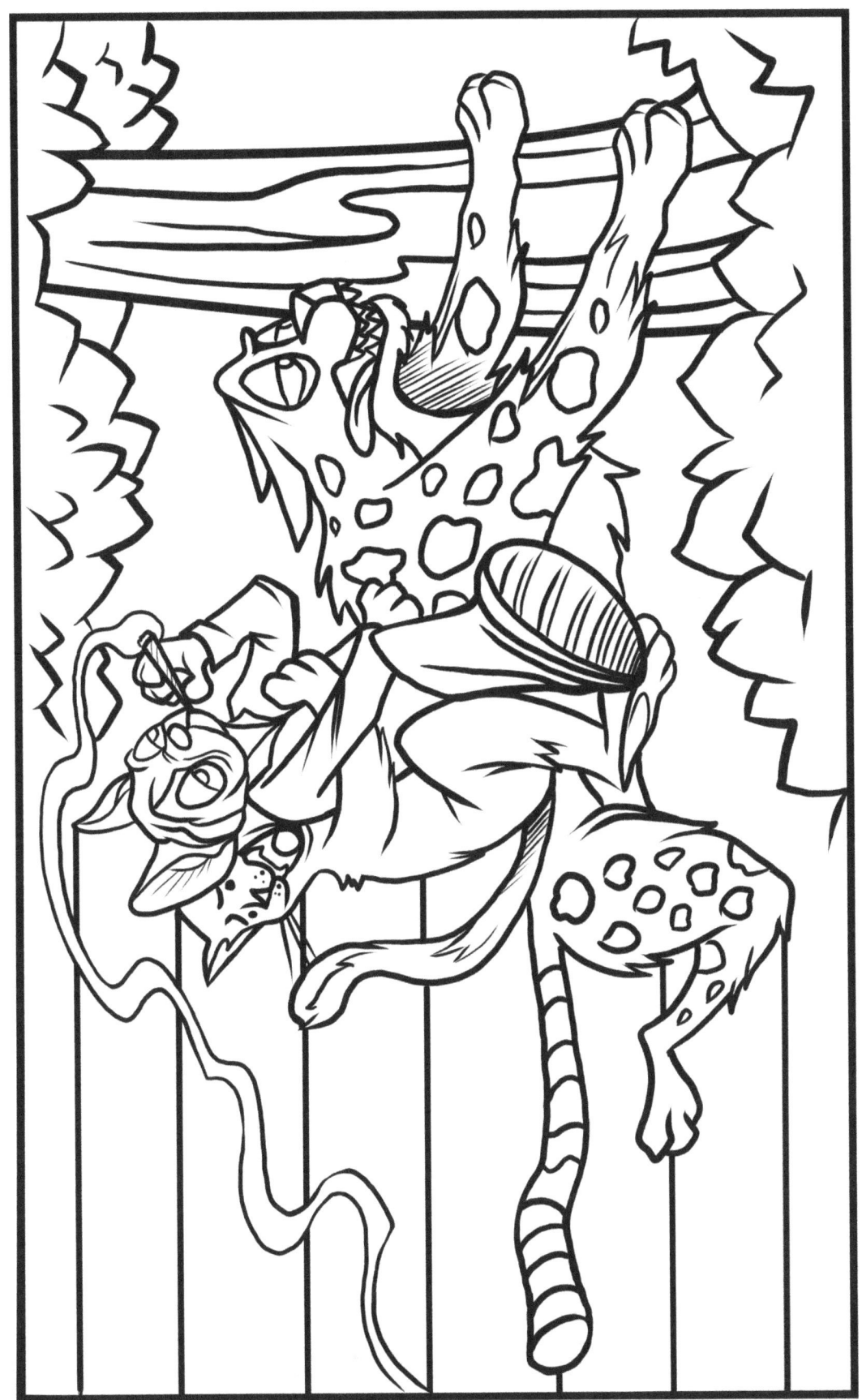

ANIMALS GETTING HIGH

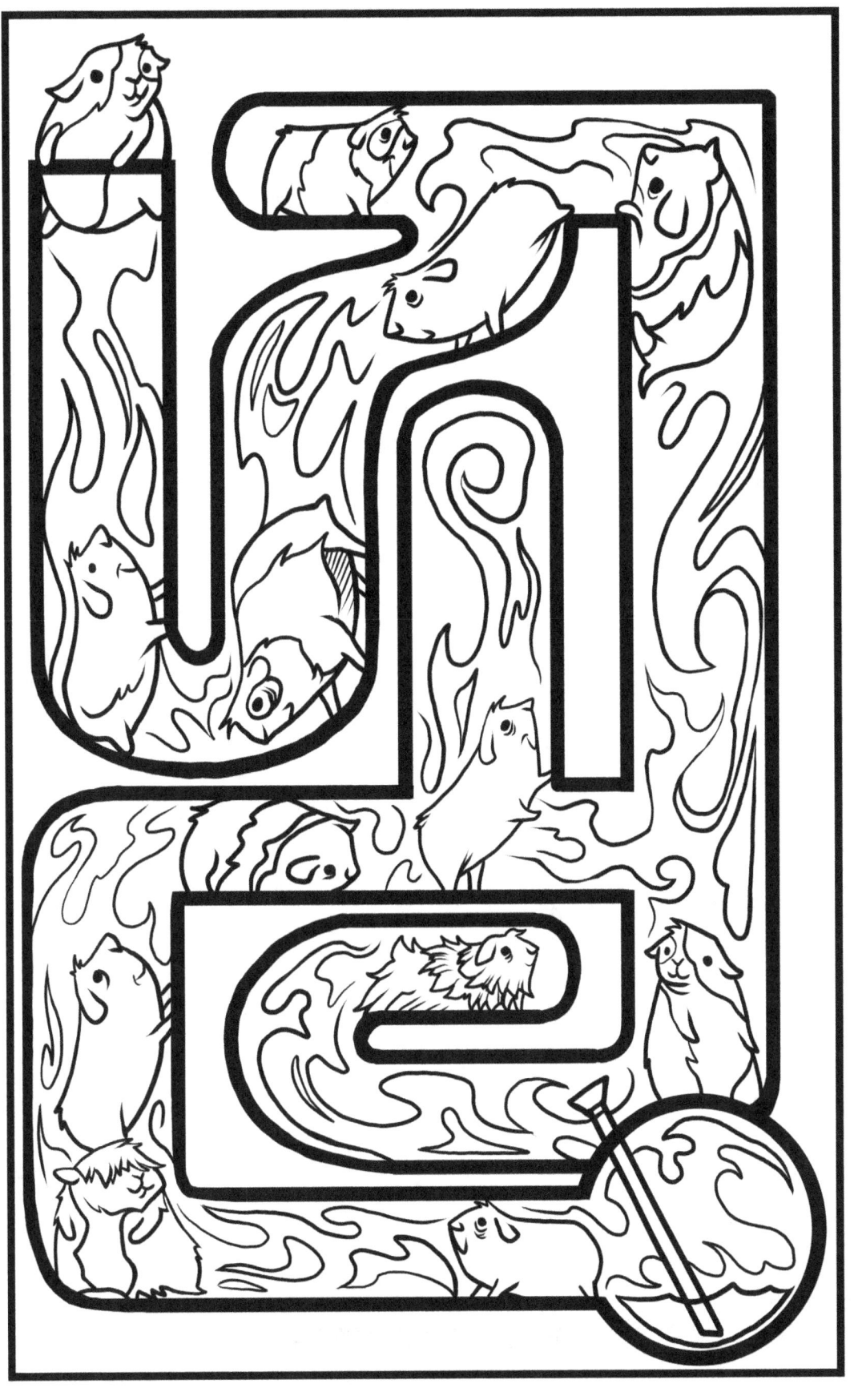

ANIMALS GETTING HIGH

ANIMALS GETTING HIGH

www.ingramcontent.com/pod-product-compliance
Lightning Source LLC
Chambersburg PA
CBHW080532220526
45465CB00006B/2682